SENTENCED TO LIVE

BY ALICIA S. JONES

"The Miracle of Genesis"

*Trust in the Lord with all thine heart; and
lean not unto thine own understanding. In all
thy ways acknowledge him, and he shall
direct thy paths. Proverbs 3:5-6 (KJV)*

Dedication

I dedicate this book to my readers. With God, all things are possible. Don't give up!

In loving memory of my sons, Cameron McKel and Christian Blair Jones; grandmother, Iceola "Madear" Hawkins-Sutton; aunts, Alice Marie, Beverly Ann, and Veronica Gayle; and brother, Jermayne.

Acknowledgments

Thank you, **God,** for giving me the vision to write this book many years ago.

To my husband, Greg:
Thank you for making everything possible and encouraging me every step of the way.

To my daughter, Genesis:
Thank you, Gen, for shaping my faith in God.

To my mother, Yvonne:
I cannot thank you enough for sacrificing your own dreams and raising me to believe that anything is possible.

To my extended family:
I am grateful for your continuous support.

To the fruitful branches of my tree trunk:
Thank you for your spiritual nourishment,
prayers, support and encouragement over
the years and wisdom with this project. My
leaves continually grow in and out of season
because of you.

*Rev. Terry Abercrombie, First Lady Florence
Boyd, Pastor J. Edgar Boyd, Linda Branch,
Marcia Brickley, Chris Broussard, Carrington
Family, Overseer Sandra Carter, California
Circle of Friends (COF), Pastor Sean Cort, My
First Cousins, Crossing Guard from Prescott
Middle, Editor Katrina Sanders, Elm Grove
Baptist Church of Baton Rouge, La, Pamala
Ellens, FAME Church of Los Angeles,
Friendship Baptist Church of Yorba Linda,
Dejuanna Harmon, Dana Harris, Helen Harris,
Tommy Harris, Debbie Holley, Linda Lampley-
Ike, Alfred and Joyce Jackson, Bettye Jackson,
Dr. Jessica Johnson, Clarence and Janice Jones,
Leora Jones, LA Mass, Areva Martin, Miller
Family, GJ Ministry, Bertha Myers, Alda*

Sentenced to Live

Nelson, Dr. Jereme Nelson, Nephews, Nieces, Praises of Zion Baptist Church of Los Angeles, Prayer Posse, Dr. and Mrs. Alfred Sloan, Southern University Alumni Los Angeles Chapter, Derek Sutton, Taylor Family, Donald Taylor, Timekeeper Deirdre Cuffie, Terry Wooten, True Perspective Publishing Staff, and Belinda Wright.

Foreword

Caring, loving, strong, and supportive are the perfect descriptions of my wife, author Alicia S. Jones. She is one of the most amazing persons I have ever encountered. I am blessed to call her my partner for life and mother of our children. *Sentenced to Live* is a personal testimony of standing in the face of fear, sickness, death, and pain and finding the courage to hold on no matter how bad things looked or felt. It is a heartfelt account of remaining steadfast in our faith and pressing forward against all odds, even when we felt like giving up. We have weathered many storms and endured many seasons, and through it all God has been right there. He has never left nor forsaken us. *Sentenced to Live* was written to give you hope. It is through these trials that we were tested, and our tests became our victory, and our victory became our testimony, and our testimony became our ministry. To God be the glory for the things He has done!

Proud Husband, Gregory G. Jones

Table of Contents

Sentenced to Live

Chapter One

Broken Optimism

In the summer of 1998, I visited my hometown in Louisiana to attend a choral reunion with my husband, Greg. Baton Rouge, known as the "Red Stick" along the Mississippi river, was living up to its name if the red stick was a match. The   smoking hot and humid air did its best to smother everyone who dared to move around outside.

During my visit home, my mother reminded me that it was the first time I had ever come home, and my monthly friend "Mary" did not appear. The only way I could convince her that I was not pregnant was to take an

at-home pregnancy test. I knew without a shadow of a doubt the test would be negative. The last thing I needed was to be pregnant.

Prior to this, Greg and I buried two sons, Cameron in 1995 and Christian in 1997. Our first pregnancy had come as a shock to everyone. My husband and I had been married for four years, and we had not conceived a child. Here I was, spreading the happy news that I was pregnant. Our entire family was extremely elated for us.

In summer 1995, I flew to Baton Rouge to attend a baby shower in my honor, planned by my family and close friends. The celebration was held at my church, Elm Grove Baptist. What fun I had that day with more than 100 guests consisting of family and friends from church, childhood, high school, and college!

Sentenced to Live

How in Jesus' name was I going to get all the gifts back to California? I don't think any of us thought of that prior to planning an out-of-state shower. But, that was a problem for later. All I wanted to do was enjoy the moment.

I was smiling and floating like a cloud in the sky, basking in the beautiful occasion. I remember wearing an emerald green dress with gold accessories and clear high heels with gold trimming. The mature women of God used to tell us that it was not good to wear heels during your pregnancy, but I wore them anyway and felt great.

As a former high school athlete, I always had strong legs so I was good. It was hot as hot sauce but I had to have on pantyhose. My grandmother and my mother would have scolded me for not wearing pantyhose with a dress. Therefore, I had to make sure they were shimmer gold Berkshire pantyhose.

Sentenced to Live

As soon as I returned from Louisiana, I received a call from my gynecologist's office at Kaiser that my doctor wanted me to have an amniocentesis because of an abnormal alpha fetoprotein (AFP) test. I really did not want to take this test because of the small risk of miscarriage. Statistics showed that it was a 1 in 200 or less chance of having a miscarriage after this procedure, but I decided to go forth with the test.

One of my cousins accompanied me to my appointment because Greg was working on an earthquake cleanup project in Northridge. I was so nervous. I kept praying over and over asking God to calm my spirit.

The test went well, but a few hours later I felt a little cramping and discomfort, which was one of the side effects. I started having second thoughts about taking the test but moved on and focused on taking great care of our baby and myself.

Sentenced to Live

A few weeks later, we received a disturbing phone call from my mother that my 39-year-old aunt went home to be with the Lord. She suffered with lupus for a very long time. My heart was aching severely for my three young cousins who were left behind without a mother. There was no way on earth that I was going to miss my aunt's funeral. My brother, who was living with us and attending college in Los Angeles, flew home with me to pay our respects to my mother's youngest sister.

It was a big shock and very difficult to see my family so devastated. I knew I had to be strong for my grandmother, mother, and cousins. My aunt was the sweetest woman; she had a heart of gold and hardly ever said no to anyone.

She knew how to do everything from changing a tire to cooking a huge batch of southern fried catfish in her cast iron skillet for a multitude. She carried on my

Sentenced to Live

grandmother's recipe of seasoning the fish
with salt, pepper, and cornmeal. That's it! It
was my favorite entree that she cooked.
Time passed so quickly during our visit.
Although it was a sad occasion, it was great
seeing family. It was time to head back to the
West Coast. I returned just in time to see
Greg minister in song with The LA Mass
Choir at their "Unconditional Love" live
recording. He had written three songs for
this particular project.

I was so proud of him. He was disappointed
that he couldn't make it to the funeral, but
flights were really expensive, and we both
felt it was best that my brother was there.
My mother-in-law and one of her friends
flew back with my brother and me to attend
the live recording.

I was so exhausted but pressed my way to
witness this spirit-filled occasion. Some of
Los Angeles' best musicians and writers also
attended the recording. It was an invitation

Sentenced to Live

only event for families of the choir members, musicians, writers, and music industry moguls. The recording was awesome, and the spirit of the Lord permeated the room. Greg was smiling as if he was receiving a Grammy award that night. He was so excited to have his material featured on a national recording label.

Sentenced to Live

Chapter Two

Cam's Flight

Sunday morning appeared quickly, and it was time to get ready for Sunday school at Praises of Zion. I learned so much in this class, which was the onset of my journaling. I wrote a prayer in my journal every day. Amazingly, there were several young women in my class who were pregnant. It was fun sharing this journey with them and attending baby shower after baby shower.

One Friday evening, I left work early because I was not feeling well. I picked up my brother from football practice and

Sentenced to Live

headed to Inglewood to our apartment. I decided to put my feet up and relax for the remainder of the evening.

Greg was preparing to leave for choir rehearsal with LA Mass, but I stayed home to make sure the baby and I were comfortable. A few minutes passed and I started to feel some pain, which persisted, then became severe. Greg and I packed my bag and headed to Kaiser Permanente Hospital in Harbor City. I was in so much pain that I could not sit properly in the car.

I was on my knees with my back facing the front windshield in our 1994 black Ford Probe. Greg was driving so fast to get me to the hospital. He carefully zoomed in and out of the lanes to navigate traffic on the 110 Freeway.

He nearly drove inside the hospital to get me as close as he could to the entrance. A few hospital staff members were standing

Sentenced to Live

outside, and he shouted, "My wife is in labor!"

They took me straight to Labor and Delivery without asking any questions. The doctors examined me immediately and prepped me for surgery. I could see Greg's face. He looked really nervous and worried and said he was calling my mom and his parents to notify them. It was our first child. I thought, *this really can't be happening to me; it's too early.* I was praying, crying, and asking God to give me strength to endure the pain. It was so unbearable.

As I prayed, a huge amount of fluid gushed from my cervical area. The anesthesiologist administered anesthesia expeditiously. I could tell, by the urgency of this delivery, that I would have to have a C-section to save little Cameron.

The mask was placed over my face, and I was out like a light. When I woke up, I was told that my placenta had ruptured. My

Sentenced to Live

uterus had separated from the placenta. It was considered a "class three characteristic," which included heavy vaginal bleeding, excruciating uterine pain, maternal shock, and fetal distress.

On September 8, 1995, I had given birth to our first son, Cameron McKel, who was three months premature. Cameron was transferred to Kaiser Bellflower NICU where he would receive better care. Greg and I visited Cameron every day. It was hard waking up every day without him at my side. I had already decided that I was going to breastfeed.

I pumped milk several times a day to keep a nice supply ready for him. He was progressing well and gaining a little weight. Every now and then, we would see a little smirk on his face as he was trying to smile.

He looked so much like Greg. We prayed over him endlessly and sang to uplift his spirit. I think he really enjoyed that. We were so thankful to the Lord for his turn around and were told that he could possibly go home within a few weeks.

On October 8, I woke up feeling horrible. I was shaking all over and felt like I was dying. I couldn't explain what was happening. I started bleeding severely and felt it was best that I go to the hospital to be observed. I kept telling Greg over and over that I felt like I was dying. He was looking at me with those big eyes like I was crazy. He said, "Bey, I'm calling your mom; you are not making any sense at all."

He called my mother and asked her to speak with me regarding what I was feeling. "Mom, I know you think I'm experiencing postpartum depression and losing it, but I feel like I'm dying," I told her.

The emergency room doctor told me that my menstrual cycle was starting again. I thought to myself, *oh my, haven't I bled enough? This is really too much.* I kept telling the doctor that I felt like something else was wrong.

He said, "Mrs. Jones, you are fine. Go home and get some rest." I begged Greg to take me to see Cameron in spite of what the doctor said. We stopped at the hospital to see Cameron on our way home and were told by his doctors that he had developed neonatal sepsis, a potentially fatal whole-body inflammation caused by severe infection. It's pretty common with a preterm delivery, as well as infected placenta tissue and amniotic fluids. Our poor son was struggling to live.

We prayed after hearing this news and called all the prayer warriors we knew, asking them to join us in prayer for our son. I was still bleeding profusely, feeling down and depressed. I knew my son was sick, but I couldn't explain exactly what I was feeling.

Sentenced to Live

Greg and I returned home after a long afternoon. We immediately got on our knees and started praying again for our son. At that time, my brother entered our room and handed me the phone, stating it was the hospital.

The doctor informed us that Cameron's condition had worsened and we needed to return to the hospital immediately. We called our parents, headed towards the door, and the phone rang. It was the hospital informing us that Cameron had passed. We called our parents to update them and then drove to the hospital in total silence.

My thoughts were all over the place. I don't know what Greg was thinking as he was driving, but I was in a complete state of shock. After Cameron passed, that feeling of death I was inexplicably experiencing disappeared.

I realized that the Lord was preparing me for my child's death. I can't begin to explain

Sentenced to Live

how that felt. It was horrible. We had so many decisions to make: which mortuary to call, casket selection, what clothes to bury Cameron in, type of service, graveside or church funeral, programs, how we would pay for it all, and so much more!

Endless questions flooded my mind. Our pastor found a local mortuary and helped us plan Cameron's graveside service. I couldn't believe that I was sitting in the mortuary planning my son's funeral at the age of 25. It was truly a traumatic time in my life. Our parents flew in for the service. I don't think any of them really knew what to say. The pressure was eased, a little, due to their presence, but it didn't take away the pain of losing our firstborn.

We received so many cards, flowers, visits, phone calls, prayers, and enough food to feed an army. I was so appreciative, but I wanted to be alone to grieve and deal with our loss. I thought of Cameron so much. I wondered how he would have looked.

I realized that I needed to seriously seek the face of my Heavenly Father to keep my sanity. I kept writing in my prayer journal, which was a form of release for me and a one-on-one conversation with God. I was pouring out my thoughts and feelings. I was extremely excited for the other ladies in my Sunday school class who were delivering healthy babies. I kept smiling and encouraging them even though my heart was ripped to pieces.

Chapter Three

Christian's Journey

At this time, I was working at Personal Involvement Center. I returned to work two months after Cameron's death during the late fall of 1995 and started a new position at Youth Intervention Center. I felt I needed a fresh start.

I didn't know anyone at the company except my new boss who had trained me for the position at my previous job. Therefore, it was easy for me to hide behind the pain because no one else knew me. A few weeks

Sentenced to Live

after returning, I met a young lady who really needed encouragement.

She was single and pregnant. I reluctantly began to share how I lost my first child. She was so attentive and wanted to hear what happened detail by detail. I had no idea how much I was helping myself by sharing. God gave me so much strength and stamina afterwards. I felt compelled to plan her baby shower at the office.

Every "i" was dotted and every "t" crossed. I wanted it to be perfect as if it was my own child. We had a huge buffet serving line with every inch of the room decorated and a gorgeous baby shower tree that was designed by a friend. There were so many gifts for the baby. Her little girl was born on Greg's birthday.

I remember it like it was yesterday. I had so much fun planning her shower, and it was a step of healing for my heart. I immediately

Sentenced to Live

began to feel like myself again. God is truly amazing!

A year later, Greg and I decided to move to Riverside County into a nice, quiet community away from the hustle and bustle of Los Angeles County. We were young and willing to commute to work and church in Los Angeles every day. It worked out well because Greg and I were able to carpool. We had a lot of time to chat during our commute. We loved our new neighborhood.

After settling in our new place for a couple of months, we decided to step out on faith and work to expand our family. I knew without a doubt the moment I was pregnant. We conceived in the winter of 1996. I was completely sure I was expecting this time.

 It was so similar to my first pregnancy with Cameron. I visited my doctor to determine how far along I was in the pregnancy. The doctor confirmed that I was six weeks pregnant.

Sentenced to Live

It didn't take long for me to realize that the commute was too much on my body and the baby. Although my husband and I carpooled, it was still overwhelming. My boss insisted that I work from home three days a week to ensure that I was getting proper rest. I visited my gynecologist quite often to stay abreast about my pregnancy.

Around the middle of the first trimester, my doctor told me that I needed to attend a class to learn how to give myself injections of heparin in my abdomen area.

"You're kidding, right?" I said to my doctor. I had a condition called thrombosis. I had to give myself heparin injections twice a day to increase the blood flow to the baby and prevent clotting.

I took it like a champ and said, "Ok, I will do whatever I can to get this child here safely." I was very uncomfortable giving myself injections while I was at work and church,

Sentenced to Live

but I knew it was important for my unborn child.

I used to transport all of my syringes and medicine supplies in a cute lunch bag, so people could not see what I was carrying. Everyone thought it was my snack pack.

During this pregnancy, my husband accepted a new job at Friendship Baptist Church in Yorba Linda, which was much closer to our home. Greg was a pianist and started on Easter Sunday in 1997.

I accompanied him to his first rehearsal with the Voices of Joy. I sat in the back of the church waiting for him to complete his rehearsal. As it ended, I started feeling a little weird. We traveled home to pick up a few things and decided to go to the hospital to make sure everything was ok.

We arrived at Kaiser Permanente Hospital in Riverside around midnight. All was well until I was asked to provide a urine sample.

Sentenced to Live

I went into the restroom, and when I looked down I saw clots of blood in the toilet. I remained calm and pushed the call button for assistance. They placed me on a monitor, and I immediately started having contractions. The doctor asked the nurse to administer magnesium sulfate to slow down the contractions. My mouth was dry, and I felt my body temperature increasing. A few hours later, I was in full-blown labor. I could not believe this was happening. I was only five months pregnant.

We called home to inform our family, prayer warriors, and friends from our former church in Los Angeles because we did not know anyone at Friendship.

I remember my previous obstetrician gynecologist telling me that it was not safe for me to go through natural birth ever in life. I asked the nurse to inform the doctors that I could not go through natural childbirth because of the previous placenta abruption pregnancy with Cameron.

During this time, I asked Greg to specifically call three women to come and pray near my room: "my mother away from home," my Sunday school teacher, and my unborn child's Godmother. By this time, my head was tilted so far back that I felt like I was standing on my head. They were doing everything they could to help me keep this little one inside.

The pain increased greatly! Our son, Christian, slipped into the birth canal. All I could do was pray, trust God, and push when the doctors instructed me to do so. The doctor said Christian would probably die immediately after delivery because it was just too early, and the hospital was not properly equipped to care for him.

I could not believe this was happening AGAIN. I was giving birth to another child with whom I would never bond. My "mother

Sentenced to Live

away from home" walked in my room singing and praying.

She held my hand and said, "I promise to stay by your side until your mother arrives from Louisiana." She prayed and sang until Christian arrived. She continued saying that God was in control, and He had great plans for my life. I was glad that everyone was there, but it was still a bleak, dark moment for me. After hours of being in labor, Christian arrived very small and fragile. He lived three to five minutes. I knew the spirit of the Lord was with me, but it was still so painful.

Once again, Greg and I planned another funeral. Mother Taylor came home with us and continued singing and praying throughout our home. Greg and I were so devastated. We had no idea how we were going to pay for another funeral.

I had only been working three days a week on my new job. We talked among ourselves

Sentenced to Live

and believed by faith that God was going to give us a plan to take care of Christian's burial. A few moments later, Mother Taylor walked into our bedroom and told Greg to sit near me. She called Papa Taylor on the phone and said she needed him to be in agreement with something that the Lord shared with her. She asked for his permission to pay for Christian's funeral. Tears began to roll down my face and the peace of God came over me so strongly. She said God gave her the message while I was giving birth to Christian.

Greg and I were blown away by this abundant blessing and rejoiced because God answered our prayers. I don't think anyone is ever prepared to bury a child, and I have never met anyone who had a life insurance policy on an unborn child.

We had the prayer of assurance and the policy was with the Lord. God already provided the coverage. Our prayers were our monthly payments. Our former pastor was not able to conduct the funeral, but Mother Taylor called one of her best friends, Rev. Searcy Jackson, to officiate the service. Greg and I did not know Rev. Jackson. He was another angel sent by God to support us in our time of need. He drove from South Central Los Angeles to Moreno Valley to take Greg to the mortuary in Inglewood and finalize Christian's funeral.

He was an amazing man of God with a huge heart. I could not believe we were going back to the cemetery to bury our second son in the same area as Cameron in the "Garden of the Little Lambs."

The sun was shining bright with a nice, soft breeze on the morning of Christian's funeral. Unfortunately, the staff from the funeral home was late arriving with Christian's remains.

Not only were they late, but they also arrived in a family car with our baby's

Sentenced to Live

casket in the front seat of the car! I thought my family and I were going to pass out. We laughed about it later because he was secured with a seat belt in the front seat. Who does that? I guess if he were placed in the trunk, I probably would have fainted. The funeral director apologized for being late, and we proceeded with the service. Rev. Jackson was a short man in stature who delivered a powerful word from the Lord.

The eulogy was beautiful, full of encouraging words to guide us to the next chapter in our lives. The graveside service was short. We were extremely grateful for family members who traveled from Louisiana. Our close friends and co-workers joined us as well.

I can't begin to tell you how great it felt to see so many people. We buried Christian in the spring on a beautiful, sunny day near his brother Cameron in Inglewood Cemetery.

After Christian's funeral, I was a bit depressed but still believed that God had a

Sentenced to Live

plan and a purpose for my life. Jeremiah 29:11 states, "For I know the plans I have for you," declares the Lord, "plans to prosper you and not to harm you, plans to give you hope and a future." This scripture gave me hope to press forward.

Incredibly, my pregnancy was at the same time as several other members from my old Sunday school class. They were enjoying their newborns or waiting for them to arrive, but Greg and I were at the cemetery again.

I handled Christian's death a little easier than Cameron's. I witnessed Greg's heart breaking into pieces right before my very eyes. He did not say much, but I sensed he was in so much pain and could not release. Sometimes, I was not sure what to say to him. We just held each other and took one day at a time to get through this great trial.

Maybe God wanted us to adopt children. I promised myself that I would NEVER get

Sentenced to Live

pregnant again. It was very difficult for me to attend baby showers or visit someone who had a newborn. I pressed my way because I wanted to get past the hurt and be able to support and rejoice with others. I remember talking with one couple that we met at Friendship Baptist Church who was very kind to us.

They were expecting a boy. The Lord told us to bless this family with all of the boys' clothing and baby items we received for our sons. Along this journey, God has allowed me to minister to so many young women. I shared my experiences with them, giving advice and tips that I found helpful.

Sentenced to Live

Chapter Four

Buckle Up

In the spring of 1998, I went home to attend my great uncle's funeral. My grandmother, Madear, asked me to accompany her to JCPenney's to find a nice outfit to wear to her brother's funeral. She was handling his death so well.

It was unbelievable! During our ride to the mall, she began telling me all about her life insurance policies. She said, "Baby, you never know when God is going to take you home."

Sentenced to Live

She spoke about her life insurance policies like we were talking about making her famous southern bread pudding. I listened carefully, then she suddenly changed the subject to boiling crawfish, turkey necks, corn on the cob, potatoes, and Louisiana Manda's smoke sausage. Madear talked about food all the time because she was a dietician at a local high school and was excited about retiring soon.

A few months later, I went back to Louisiana to attend a choral reunion musical that Greg was conducting. We were always traveling to a music event or family gathering.

My mom kept asking me if I was pregnant, and I continually said, "No, I am not" during our visit in the Bayou. After returning to Los Angeles, I took a pregnancy test just to satisfy her and prove her wrong. Of course, it was negative and I was so excited that I wasn't.

Sentenced to Live

She called me a few weeks later and told me that she dreamed about eating some fried catfish. Well, in the South, having a dream about fish meant that someone was expecting a child. I decided to take another test to prove her wrong again; lo and behold, it was positive. The stick had double lines!

So, here I am pregnant with our third child. I thought, *what can I do to make this pregnancy different?* I felt so good about this pregnancy! Things changed so much for us. We both were working in Orange County and living in Corona.

It was a shorter drive and easier commute to work, home, and church. One beautiful Saturday evening, Greg and I attended our pastor's anniversary banquet. We were so thrilled about the pregnancy. Pastor and Sister Carrington were also extremely excited.

Pastor kept saying our baby was a miracle from God and was going to be fine. He

Sentenced to Live

introduced me to Dr. Alfred "Deacon" Sloan who was a gynecologist and deacon at our church. I did not think that there were any old school doctors left in the United States.

Dr. Sloan told everyone in his office to treat me extra special because I was the Minister of Music's wife at his church. He instructed me to see him once a week to stay on top of things. He took so many different tests to find out why I kept going into labor at the end of the second trimester.

After numerous tests, we found out that I had an incompetent cervix. It took four years and the loss of two children to determine the reason. One afternoon while conducting a seminar at work, I began feeling a little weird.

I went to the restroom during break and noticed that I was spotting. I immediately called Dr. Sloan, and he told me to head to St. Jude Medical Center in Fullerton. He

Sentenced to Live

instructed me to take a few days off work and stay off my feet to regain my strength.

I started feeling better after a few days and went back to work. During this time, I was an active member of the Women's Ministry praise team, Radiance. I was excited about the upcoming Women's Conference that's held every year in October. I was studying the music, making sure I knew the lyrics and every soprano note. As the date of the event approached, I called Dr. Sloan to remind him that I was attending the Women's Conference.

He said, "No, you are not going to the Conference, Sister Jones; I need you to rest in the afternoon after work and on the weekends."

I begged him over and over and he continued saying, "NO, Sister Jones, you are not going to that Conference." He did not think it was a good idea for me to be singing and standing on my feet continuously.

Sentenced to Live

I agreed with him but was crushed because I really wanted to go. God always has a reason for doing things and often reveals why later. While sitting at my desk on the first day of the conference, I began thinking about my sisters in Christ and wishing I were there singing with Radiance. I received a phone call from the receptionist that my husband was at the front desk. I asked her to send him back. He got on his knees and told me that he had some really bad news to share with me.

I kept saying, "What is it, Greg?" over and over. He was speechless and having a difficult time trying to get his words together. His eyes were filled with tears. So, I began asking questions. I said, "Did you lose your job?" He said, "No."

I continued with more questions. Finally, I realized that I needed to be silent and give him time to form his words. He told me that my grandmother, Madear, had passed away

Sentenced to Live

in Baton Rouge. I was completely shocked and in great disbelief. I picked up the phone immediately and called my mother.

I said, "Mom, it's me (as if she didn't recognize my voice). Is it true? Did she die? Oh my God, not Madear." She began to cry, and my cousin took the phone to explain what happened. Tears began to roll down my face. I could not believe what was happening. I had an instant flashback of the conversation Madear and I had in the car on our way to JCPenney's to purchase a suit for my great uncle's funeral.

I remembered everything she said about her life insurance policies. Greg drove me home after delivering the news. I was crying quietly all the way home. After we arrived, I started calling airlines, searching for bereavement flight deals.

I suddenly realized I had not told Dr. Sloan about my travel plans. I called him and shared what happened. He was very quiet

Sentenced to Live

while I was speaking. Afterwards, he said, "Alicia, I'm very sorry to hear that your grandmother passed. I don't think it's a good idea to fly in your condition."

I said, "Dr. Sloan, you don't understand. She is the only grandmother I have. I need to be there with my mother and family."

He said, "It's a strong possibility that you could have a miscarriage if you get on that plane. I understand, but I don't think it's a good idea." I cried for hours.

I could not believe that I would not be at Madear's homegoing celebration. I called my mom to let her know what Dr. Sloan recommended, and she agreed that I should take it easy and stay in California.

It felt like a piece of my heart had fallen to the bottom of the ocean with no return. All I could think about was not seeing her face again or calling her just to chat about

Sentenced to Live

cooking tips, recipes, and everything under the sun.

I knew we would eventually see each other again in Heaven. Surely, God had his arms stretched wide receiving the dynamic soprano and cook into the pearly gates singing "There Will Be Peace in the Valley." That was her favorite song. She enjoyed hearing my father-in-law sing this song in church, so it was fitting that he sang it at her celebration. I was sad because Madear was so excited about my pregnancy, and I wanted my child to know her great-grandmother who taught me so much about cooking.

I was like a sponge soaking it all up since I was a little girl. I cooked my first Thanksgiving dinner when I was in middle school. I thought my mother was crazy for forcing me to do it, but I thank God for those days now because my husband loves to eat.

Sentenced to Live

A few days passed, and I contacted my cousin to submit a poem for the obituary on behalf of the grandchildren. She thought it was a great idea. I needed to do something to feel like I was a part of Madear's homegoing celebration.

Greg flew home to attend the service on our behalf, and this brought me some relief. A group of friends from our local church visited me the day of the funeral and brought food, flowers, and cards, but it didn't fill the empty hole in my heart. I called my mother and grandmother's home every hour to see if they had returned from the funeral. The majority of my family lived in the same neighborhood, and our church was only blocks away on the same street.

I was so concerned about my mom. I knew God's angels were surrounding her with comfort, but I wanted to be there to support her. Everyone told me that her celebration of life was absolutely beautiful.

Chapter Five

Amazing Love

The pain subsided day by day, and I went back to work. I was still being cautious, following Dr. Sloan's instructions. Thanksgiving was around the corner, and I couldn't cook anything. A friend called to tell me that her mother cooked Thanksgiving dinner for us, and I was thrilled. About a week after Thanksgiving, I started spotting again.

Since we were living in the Inland Empire, Dr. Sloan suggested that we move to Orange County to be closer to his office and the hospital where he would deliver the baby. We moved to an affordable, nice-and-small two-bedroom apartment in North Orange County.

Ironically, our new home was walking distance to my job. God's favor was upon us. A month later, Dr. Sloan suggested a cervical cerclage, which is a procedure that stitches the cervix to help prevent a miscarriage. I followed his recommendation and had the minor procedure at Placentia Linda Hospital. It went smoothly.

I was awake during the procedure; however, everything below my waist was completely numb. Dr. Sloan talked to me the entire time. I thought to myself, *this guy always has a conversation tucked in his pocket.* Of course, the conversation had nothing to do with babies or the procedure he was performing. He loved to talk about Bible stories.

I took a few days off before returning to work. I tried to go on with life as usual;

Sentenced to Live

however, it became more interesting as the weeks progressed.

 After a few episodes of spotting, Dr. Sloan restricted me to complete bed rest. I was confined to bed for six long months. I could not go anywhere. My weekly outing was a visit to Dr. Sloan's office. I was allowed to sit up in the living room twice each day for a few minutes.

Joyce, the director of Christian education at Friendship Baptist Church, sent inspirational books home with Greg and encouraged me to read them frequently. The devotions kept me rooted, grounded, and focused. It was an experience I will never forget.

Four other young ladies in my church were also pregnant. Babies were booming like crazy! Greg and I were so blessed to have great friends. Various deaconesses (Sis. Lorna, Sis. Nancy, Sis. Punkin, and Sis. Reed) brought us food a couple of days each week.

Sentenced to Live

Greg cooked breakfast for me every morning before he left for work. Some of my sisters from the church stopped by during their lunch breaks or days off and brought me some of my favorite things to eat. They also assisted with whatever we needed. On weekends, my girlfriend, Katrina B., would bring buffalo wings with celery sticks and pecan praline pie for dessert from Denny's. This was the highlight of my week. I ate very healthy; however, I was allowed to splurge sparingly.

This time, the pregnancy was progressing well. It was time to find out the baby's sex, and Greg and I were coming up with all kinds of names. Everyone thought it would be another boy.

There were no granddaughters on either side of our families. My sister-in-law, Tracy, was also pregnant and did not know the sex of her baby. Lo and behold, we both were

Sentenced to Live

having girls. Our daughters would be the first girls born on both sides of the family.

I was so excited! Greg and I wanted our daughter's name to be meaningful, so we began researching names and their meanings. I spent a lot of time reading and meditating to our baby, as she turned somersaults, kicked, and stretched in my belly, reminding me that she was a fighter. I read stories to her every day to make sure she knew my voice.

After deliberating, I selected the name Genesis because it is the first book in the Bible. It signifies a new beginning. She would be our first daughter and our parents' first granddaughter.

She would have the first initial of God and her father, Greg. For all of these reasons, Greg loved the name as much as I did. Every afternoon, Genesis would leap in my belly when it was time for Greg to come home.

Sentenced to Live

It was the strangest thing. Somehow, she sensed her dad's presence. She was spiritually connected to him from the womb. We consistently laughed about how I knew when Greg was on his way home, even before he called.

Chapter Six

Preparing for the Princess

The pregnancy continued to go exceptionally well, and we were so excited that this experience was so much better than the previous two pregnancies. Dr. Sloan complimented us on how well everything was going and how healthy the baby was developing.

Greg and I were so happy, and Genesis was excited too, as she was having herself a Holy Ghost party inside my womb. She moved when we spoke to her and leaped on many

Sentenced to Live

occasions when we sang songs or played music. We had a happy and active little girl.

I arrived at the end of my second trimester without any issues or concerns. Praise the Lord! Our friends from Los Angeles and Orange Counties planned a co-ed baby shower at the Anaheim Community Center, which was very close to our home. I had never witnessed a baby shower planned so extravagantly.

The invitations and decorations were so elegant and dainty. Our friends selected a Minnie Mouse theme. There were several hundred attendees. This was truly a celebration of the miracle of Baby Genesis.

The menu included grilled chicken pasta with a choice of marinara or alfredo sauce, a green salad, bread, and mouthwatering cake for dessert. The hostesses' husbands served the guests so that no one would have to stand in line.

Sentenced to Live

They served with such sweet spirits. It was a breath of fresh air. The ladies were keeping things flowing by preparing the plates for the guys to serve, seating guests, and accepting and placing gifts on the designated tables. They also coordinated the games and kept guests comfortable. We had a blast but were on a tight schedule to ensure Dr. Sloan did not show up and shut the entire party down for not following his instructions.

Genesis' room was full of wonderful gifts. She had everything she needed.

I was approaching 35 weeks when something suddenly changed. While lying in bed, I felt a few contractions. I called my husband and Dr. Sloan to let them know. Dr. Sloan instructed me to have Greg bring me to the hospital, along with my bag, in case I needed to stay overnight.

I had a strong intuition that I was not going back home that night. Upon arrival, Dr. Sloan informed me that I was going to be admitted

Sentenced to Live

at Placentia Linda Hospital until the baby arrived. I didn't argue with him. I had reached 35 weeks, so whatever he said do I was going to do it. He removed the cervical cerclage and the contractions subsided.

I continued resting in the hospital for the next couple of weeks. Greg set up a VCR and brought me every videotape that he owned. My hospital room was beginning to look like our bedroom.

The hospital staff was exceptionally nice and welcoming. Greg and I didn't want anyone at the hospital with us during the delivery time. So many people had already done so much, and we didn't want to worry or overwhelm anyone.

Our church membership was several thousand, so you can imagine the number of people who were calling and offering their assistance. It was refreshing but sometimes overwhelming. Whenever someone asked to help, I answered, "No, I don't need anything, and you don't have to come. We are doing great," which was the truth. Nevertheless, one of my friends stopped by on April 19. During her visit, I received a call from two friends, Joyce and Katrina B., asking if they could come to the hospital. Again, I said, "Don't worry about us, we are fine. I promise to call if something changes." Well, neither of them listened. Joyce showed up with more reading material. Soon after, Katrina showed up with her list of folks to contact when the baby arrived.

I informed them that Dr. Sloan induced labor. We picked April 19 as her birthday from the list of dates Dr. Sloan gave us. Those who know me can confirm that I am an organized, neat freak.

I had all instructions written concisely and clearly. Katrina B. was scheduled to call two of my friends, Katrina M. and Sharon, to ask them to contact our friends in Los Angeles County and update them on the status.

Sentenced to Live

Chapter Seven

Labor and Delivery

I went for a short stroll through the hospital with Katrina B and Joyce. We were laughing and talking when all of sudden I felt this ginormous pain hit the bottom of my stomach. It didn't feel like contractions.

I told them that I needed a wheelchair quickly because I felt myself falling to floor. Simultaneously, my water broke, blood was flowing, and I lost all control of my bowels. My heart was racing a mile a minute.

Sentenced to Live

I was nervous but felt confident that all was going to be well. I remained calm because I didn't want to do anything to hurt Genesis. Greg was waiting back in the hospital room.

He had no idea what was going on until Katrina B. notified him something went wrong during our stroll down the hall. The nurses rushed me to Labor and Delivery. Dr. Sloan walked in and asked, "What happened?" I told him that I walked down the hall, and everything went crazy. He was calm, but I could tell by the look on his face that he was very concerned. He told Greg to scrub up and get ready to see his baby girl.

He also told the ladies to call Pastor Carrington and tell him to get here fast and pray hard. I overheard them saying that Genesis' fetal heart tones were at 50 and dropped to 0. A few moments later, he said, "Bro. Greg, unfortunately, I cannot allow you to be in the delivery room at this time."

Sentenced to Live

Our written plan of the delivery was altered. My uterus had ruptured into pieces. Help me, Jesus! I knew it was serious. Everyone was moving so fast. It was as if a category five hurricane had landed in Labor and Delivery.

Dr. Sloan was telling the anesthesiologist to hurry up and get me sedated so he could get things going. I felt the knife for about two seconds and remember going into la la land. While I was under anesthesia, Madear came to me in my dream and began speaking to me. She said, "Fight, fight, fight! God has not given you the spirit of fear; but of power, love, and a sound mind. Keep saying it over and over. It is going to be alright." I guess I was in the middle of transitioning in and out. It felt like I was under anesthesia forever, but I was told the delivery only took 10 minutes.

Dr. Sloan called Dr. So, a pediatrician from St. Jude, to assist. Dr. So arrived five to seven

Sentenced to Live

minutes after the birth. At this time, the respiratory therapist had already intubated Genesis with a 4.0 tube. Genesis was not breathing.

Dr. So performed cardiopulmonary resuscitation (CPR) continuously for 15-20 minutes, while we were still in the operating room. Genesis' Apgar scores were 1 and 1. According to Kids Health (2018), Apgar stands for **A**ppearance (skin color), **P**ulse (heart rate), **G**rimace response (reflexes), **A**ctivity (muscle tone) and **R**espiration (breathing rate and effort). The score is obtained by adding points (2, 1 or 0) for each of the five areas. It is administered twice, one minute after birth and five minutes after birth.

The best possible Apgar score is 10 and 10. Genesis was not in a good place. Placentia Linda Hospital did not have a NICU and was unable to provide the immediate care that

Sentenced to Live

Genesis needed; she was transported to St. Jude Hospital in Fullerton.

After the delivery, I assumed that I would be taken to recovery for a short while. However, I heard Dr. Sloan call my name and say, "Alicia, can you hear me? You did well. You lost a lot of blood.

We may have to administer a blood transfusion. You went through a lot, young lady. Genesis is really ill, but she is a fighter like her mother. She suffered a lack of oxygen to her brain due to your uterus rupturing. I was able to repair your uterus. She was transferred to St. Jude in Fullerton a couple of miles away."

Dr. So accompanied Genesis in the ambulance to St. Jude, which has an awesome neonatal intensive care unit. "Don't worry, they will take good care of her," Dr. So stated.

Sentenced to Live

Dr. Sloan said, "Greg, Pastor Carrington and others are waiting outside this door to greet you. It's going to be ok." I was still out of it, so I don't think everything was really registering.

I went from Recovery to my room. Greg, Joyce, Katrina, Sheryl and Pastor Carrington were still there. I could tell something was really wrong with Genesis because everyone was so quiet and very cautious with his or her words.

Pastor Carrington said, "Poppee is here." The look on Greg's face said it all in a nutshell. Someone took a picture of Genesis and showed it to me. Our beautiful little girl was swollen and plump. She arrived on Monday, April 19 at 9:42 p.m., weighing 5 pounds 15 ounces and measured 18 ½ inches long. Her skin was glowing and her hair was beautiful.

I eventually fell asleep and woke up a few times during the night, feeling very drowsy.

Sentenced to Live

Morning came, everyone was gone, meds had worn off a little, pain was intense, and reality kicked into high gear. It all started to make sense that I was really ill and so was my daughter.

We were in two different hospitals approximately six miles apart. At some point, I asked Greg for an update on Genesis. He said, "Our daughter is in very bad shape.

Her brain is severely damaged. The brain stem is the only part that is functioning, per the doctor. She has tubes everywhere and is not breathing on her own." Tears began to roll down my face. I said, "Well, Bey, we are going to trust God. He did not bring her this far to take her away." I wanted to see her so badly, but I couldn't. I asked Greg what time he was going to St. Jude to be at Genesis' side.

He said, "I can't do it; I don't want to get attached to her and something happens. I'm sorry, Bey, I don't think I can do it." Of

Sentenced to Live

course, that was fear talking, and his heart was hurting.

Cameron passed away, Christian passed away, and it was a strong possibility that Genesis could pass away. Only the Lord could help us. This was a lot to digest. I remember two other friends, Chris and Dee, sitting quietly but offering words of encouragement periodically that night.

I had a pretty light breakfast and lunch that day. If my memory serves me correctly, the hospital staff brought us a candlelight steak and shrimp dinner for two our second night after the delivery. The dinner was presented in such a romantic manner. It was a tradition for new parents. Our friend Chris asked if he could have some. He was trying to make us laugh. However, he ate most of the meal, as I really did not have an appetite.

Our phone was ringing so much that the hospital operator called Dr. Sloan and asked if we were celebrities. Now, that was funny!

Sentenced to Live

She told him that I was receiving too many phone calls, and she was having a hard time trying to keep up.

Dr. Sloan was certain that I was not getting any rest. He had my phone calls restricted to parents only. I did not get upset; he was only looking out for us. I knew that getting extra rest would promote healing in my body.

Sentenced to Live

Chapter Eight

Just the Beginning

The time had come for me to be discharged. My mom arrived from Louisiana the day before my departure. She assisted us with packing our clothes, cards, and flowers.

Greg disconnected his VCR and neatly packed his power cords and videos that we watched to pass the time during our stay. As we were exiting the hospital, my mom shared a message with me from one of her coworkers; it was the school crossing guard in Baton Rouge.

Sentenced to Live

She said, "Ms. Sutton, I'm praying for your granddaughter. God said she shall live and not die and proclaim what the Lord has done, Psalm 118:17."

These were very powerful words from someone who lived thousands of miles away but connected to us in the spirit. The sun was shining bright as I walked slowly to the car parked near the door. It was a beautiful day in Placentia with a nice, soothing breeze blowing across my face. I got in the car, put my seatbelt on, and we headed to St. Jude to see our little princess.

We arrived at the NICU, excited about seeing Gen. Her nurses made us scrub our arms, hands, and nails before entering the unit. We put on gowns and went to see our little girl. She had a small, pink bow in her hair.

She was connected to a ventilator with tubes in her nose and IVs in her little hand. She didn't open her eyes much. The nurses told us that numerous tests had been conducted.

The head of the NICU, Dr. Madden, introduced himself and asked how I was doing.

He said, "I heard you had a pretty rough time; you are a lucky young lady. I have been taking care of your daughter. She's having a tough time as you can see and is not breathing on her own. Test results show that she is blind and deaf. Baby Jones developed seizure activity and was started on phenobarbital and Dilantin. Both are epileptic medications that are used to control seizures."

Several electroencephalograms (EEG's), a measurement of brain activity, including death in someone who is in a persistent coma (Mayo Clinic, 2018), were abnormal, indicating extensive seizure activity.

Seizures are periods of unusual brain behavior, sensations, and sometimes loss of awareness (Mayo, 2018). Genesis underwent an Auditory Brainstem Response

(ABR) test, which estimates hearing sensitivity and identifies neurological abnormalities.

It showed no responses below 40 dB, visually evoked potentials were also abnormal, indicating severe encephalopathy, a broad term for any brain disease that alters the brain's function and structure (Mayo, 2018). These waveforms normally occur within a 10-millisecond time period after a click stimulus presented at high intensities (70-90 dB normal hearing level [NHL]) (Emedicine, 2017). Doctors eventually started Genesis on feedings, but she had poor sucking and swallowing.

"Oral feedings were administered by gavage, forced feeding through a tube leading down her throat to her stomach," Dr. Madden explained. I heard what he said, but I felt like I was dreaming. That was a lot of information.

Sentenced to Live

Genesis' outer appearance was perfect. She had a beautifully shaped head, and her arms, legs, feet, hands, nose, ears, lips, face, and skin all looked normal. However, her brain was severely damaged.

I was unable to visit long and had to go home and rest, per doctor's orders. Greg and I prayed with Genesis and headed home. It was a quiet drive. I was glad to be back in my own bed but couldn't believe that my daughter and I were miles apart, and she was hospitalized in critical condition. The first thing I wanted to do upon arriving was take a shower in my own bathroom.

As I stepped into the shower, my emotions got the best of me. I cried out to the Lord, sobbing and asking, "God, why God? Why me again? Why would you allow me to progress to 37 weeks and let all of this occur?"

A crystal-clear voice spoke to me and said, "Why not you? You asked to be used for the Lord's service. How can you minister and

Sentenced to Live

encourage others if you have nothing to minister about?

Continue to study my word, pray, and I will guide you." Oooooooookaaayyy. Whew! This is a tough one, God, but we are not giving up on her. I had been reading and studying my Bible intensely during my entire pregnancy. God was up to something! We shared what Dr. Madden told us about Genesis' condition with our family, pastor, and closest friends. The "Prayer Posse" from our church visited Genesis at St. Jude several times a week and prayed. They put their hands on the glass as they prayed, as a gesture of laying hands on her physical body. Our entire congregation was praying, fasting, and interceding for Genesis.

The hospital called and informed us that some parents were upset because people were putting their hands on the windows and praying. I guess they felt it was a little disturbing. I'm sure it made some parents

Sentenced to Live

uncomfortable. Of course, the prayer warriors meant no harm; they were not only praying for Genesis but also for all of the babies in NICU.

Greg and I called the hospital several times every day to check on Genesis, even after we visited. Each time we called, the nurses were extremely patient and nice. Early one morning, we received a call from Dr. Sloan informing us that Dr. Madden wanted to meet with us in person. Greg, Mom, and I went to the hospital. Dr. Sloan was present.

Dr. Madden told us that there was nothing else they could do for Genesis, that she had been on a ventilator too long, and they would be taking her off very soon. He said, "Go home and talk to your families."

Dr. Sloan interjected and said, "Madden are you sure you have done everything possible for this baby? These young parents have buried two children within the last four years."

Sentenced to Live

Dr. Madden responded, "Yes, we've done all we can do Sloan, and the parents need to make a decision about reviving her if she stops breathing once we take her off the ventilator.

In addition, if she does begin to breathe on her own, the parents may want to consider placing the child in a special facility. Her needs are too complicated to take her home." We already knew what we were going to do but allowed Pastor Carrington and Sis. C. to come over and pray with us. We did not want our daughter to suffer.

We believed if it were God's will she would begin breathing on her own when they took her off the ventilator. We signed the documents, giving our consent to remove Genesis from the ventilator.

Genesis was almost one-week-old when the doctors decided to "try" her off the vent to see how she would respond. Our little miracle started breathing on her own! Her breathing sounded so rough and raspy.

She kept improving but had some bumpy moments. I spoke with Nurse Shelli, a NICU nurse who attended our church, about Genesis' condition to get her professional opinion.   Shelli said, "If we can get Genesis past 18 hours breathing on her own, the rest is going to be a piece of cake." Greg and I visited Genesis late one evening and met one of the night shift nurses who had fallen head over heels in love with Genesis.

This nurse took pictures and drew different animated characters and incorporated captions under the pictures. It was colorful and unique.

 She created a scrapbook for Genesis to explain each day what was going on in various pictures. My favorite page in the book was on April 28. The nurse had drawn a beautiful picture of Minnie Mouse smiling, with Genesis' weight listed as 5 pounds, 12.7

Sentenced to Live

ounces and age 9 days old. Other pages
included pictures of Genesis without the
ventilator.

It was 14 hours post extubation (without
ventilator). The caption under her next
picture read, "Hmm, what do I do now?
Where is my tube? Am I missing something?
Yay, I am not connected to my friend, the
vent." It got more exciting. The very next
day was the first time we had an
opportunity to hold her. It was April 29. Her
eyes were closed most of the time, but we
didn't care. She continued having a hard
time but was progressing. Her eyes were
opening more, but we were told, once again,
that she did not have any vision.

I always felt like she was looking straight
into my heart. We didn't let any of that
discourage us. We kept praying and
believing God for her complete healing.
Unfortunately, she was placed back and
forth on the ventilator.

Sentenced to Live

On May 27, 1999, Genesis had bloody stools, a swollen abdomen, and her x-rays revealed signs compatible with necrotizing enterocolitis(NEC), a gastrointestinal disease that mostly affects premature infants. NEC involves infection and inflammation that causes destruction of the bowel, intestines or part of the bowel.

Although it affects only 1 in 2,000 to 4,000 births, or between 1% and 5% of neonatal intensive care unit (NICU) admissions, NEC is the most common and serious gastrointestinal disorder among hospitalized preterm infants (1999 St. Jude NICU). The doctors started her on two antibiotics – ampicillin and gentamicin.

The pediatric gastroenterologist consulted and recommended a percutaneous endoscopic gastrostomy (PEG), a procedure where a flexible feeding tube is placed through the abdominal wall and into the stomach. PEG allows nutrition, fluids,

Sentenced to Live

and/or medications to be put directly into the stomach, bypassing the mouth and esophagus" (American Society for Gastrointestinal Endoscopy, 2018, para. 1). They planned to transfer Genesis to Children's Hospital of Orange County (CHOC) for this procedure.

Just a few days later, Dr. Cameron from St. Jude attempted a femoral and PIC line (peripherally inserted central catheter), but these were unsuccessful.

He spoke with us extensively and strongly recommended transferring Genesis to the NICU at CHOC as soon as possible due to severe intravenous (IV) problems.

Chapter Nine

Home Sweet Home

G enesis was transferred to CHOC on May 31 for a central line placement,

which went well. However, Genesis had several apnea episodes during the procedure. Her eyes were open with random movement but no visual response. Dr. Jotterland, from Long Beach Memorial Hospital, was called in to examine Genesis' eyes.

We were told that Genesis had cortical blindness due to occipital asphyxia and

Sentenced to Live

would most likely be totally blind. In the midst of hearing the detailed information regarding Genesis' sight, we observed an abundance of oral secretions in her mouth.

They started her on a low dose of robinul, which is used to decrease secretions via IV, and she continued to desaturate where the amount of oxygen in a baby's red blood cells decreases (Sparrow Health System, 2018). She was spitting up a lot as well. The acid in her stomach was causing this to happen. On Sunday, June 6, the nurse was making her rounds while the occupational therapist was in her room. They noticed that Genesis' eyes were moving as if she was looking at different things in the room.

The therapist held a red, black, and white chart in her hand and moved it from side to side, up and down. Genesis was following it periodically.

Her therapist was not sure of the extent of what she was seeing. The nurse called Dr.

Sentenced to Live

Jotterland to explain what she observed and to schedule an examination. She arrived later that afternoon and examined Genesis' eyesight.

Genesis was following briefly and responding to light. Hallelujah! God is so good! The diagnosis changed from cortical blindness to delayed visual maturation. I shouted, "Praise the Lord" and didn't care who heard me!

In the midst of rejoicing, several obstacles surfaced on June 20. Genesis received a blood transfusion for a hemoglobin of 8.3 and hematocrit of 24.9.

Genesis was not handling the feedings well and was having recurring regurgitation and desaturating episodes. She spit up breast milk constantly from NG feedings through her nose and mouth.

The gastroenterologist recommended that she have a fundoplication and tube

Sentenced to Live

gastrostomy to help with her acid reflux and feeding. A fundoplication prevents stomach contents from returning to the esophagus.

This operation is accomplished by wrapping the upper portion of the stomach around the lower portion of the esophagus, tightening the outlet of the esophagus as it empties into the stomach (University of San Francisco, 2018). The surgery was performed on June 22 and was very successful. She only lost about a teaspoon of blood, which is equivalent to five cubic centimeters.

Genesis was tolerating my breast milk well and started gaining weight. Blue dye was placed in her feeds for a couple of days to evaluate for any reflux. There was none noted, so the blue dye was stopped. Doctors decided not to resume any reflux medications.

Look at God! Genesis continued to improve. Little obstacles kept arising, but we

Sentenced to Live

continued standing and believing God for new miracles daily.

Late one evening, while one of the nurses was making her rounds, she observed Genesis' eye twitching with desaturations. Genesis was already receiving phenobarbital, and dosages were increased.

I really felt that the desaturations were happening due to the chloral hydrate that was given to help relieve irritation at night. She cried a lot at night. I think she cried when she knew we were not there. Her cries were music to my ears.

After tons of conversations with various doctors, therapists, and social workers, it was time for Genesis to go home. Yes, HOME, SWEET HOME. We were asked again if we wanted to place Genesis in a medical institution so she could be cared for around the clock.

Sentenced to Live

There was no way we were placing our miracle from God in an institution. That was not God's will. We knew our constant love and care would take her to great levels.

On July 2 (two days before my 29th birthday), we received an overwhelming discharge summary to take our little miracle home! It contained six different diagnoses in the summarization: hypoxic ischemic encephalopathy, gastroesophageal reflux status post fundoplication and gastrostomy tube, visual immaturity, failed visual evoked potential, failed hearing and development delay, necrotizing enterocolitis resolved, and seizures.

On top of all of that, we had to follow up with the Regional Center, gastroenterologist, speech and hearing departments for the possibility of hearing aids and an ophthalmologist at different times post discharge.

Sentenced to Live

The discharge supplies alone were like taking the entire NICU unit with us. We had to get a suction machine, French catheters, feeding syringes, saline, formula, apnea monitor, and schedule continuous physical therapy.

Bringing our daughter home was the best birthday present a mother could ever receive! Greg and I were super prepared for her departure.

July 2 would be the very first day that Genesis would see and feel sunlight, inhale outside air, travel in her car seat, and so much more. I was both excited and nervous. I wanted her first day home to be perfect.

It was our turn to be full time nurses to our daughter. I wrote out a daily to-do list, so I would not forget anything and had instantly become an over-protective mother. We decided that we would set a schedule so the two of us would not wear down too fast.

Sentenced to Live

We took turns getting up in the middle of the night. Whosever night it was, we had to rise and shine to take care of the princess. Our journey was really just beginning.

Genesis was lying so peacefully in her beautiful, white basinet near our bed. Her breathing was still labored. She had an apnea monitor attached at all times, and the feeding tube taped to her stomach.

We wanted her to feel as comfortable as if she were in her basinet at the hospital. We tried to put her between us once. That didn't work; she preferred sleeping alone. Most nights we watched her sleep because we wanted to make sure we heard the Graco baby monitor and were able to suction her to keep her nose and mouth cleared.

I spent an entire day writing down the list of follow-up appointments that we needed to schedule with specialty physicians. Our first appointment was with her pediatrician, Dr. So. We needed referrals to see all of her

Sentenced to Live

specialists. Greg had missed so many workdays that he had to get back into the swing of things a few days before her first appointment. I held down the fort during the day, and Greg and I alternated on the night shift and weekends. Teamwork! One of the deaconesses from our church, Lorna, accompanied Genesis and me to her first appointment.

Genesis seemed very comfortable on the drive to her pediatrician's appointment and was pretty quiet during our journey. As we were waiting in the examination room, Dr. So walked in. I introduced Genesis and myself.

She said, "I know who she is. I revived her for 15-20 minutes and assisted with her transfer to St. Jude." I laughed to myself. I guess she was thinking, *how could I forget this little girl who had me working so hard a few months ago?*

Sentenced to Live

I instantly fell in love with Dr. So. She was very stern but knew exactly what we needed to do to keep Genesis healthy and strong. We returned home with a list of referrals and our homework assignments for the next two days. Our first specialty appointment was with Dr. Downey.

He placed Genesis' fundoplication and a gastrostomy tube. Genesis was improving, gaining weight, less irritable, and was sleeping better at night. Dr. Downey ordered a balloon gastrostomy tube for her and placed it a couple of weeks later.

There were so many more doctors to visit, but we had to see Dr. Waki, an ENT (ears, nose, throat) specialist near St. Jude. This appointment was special in many facets. Genesis drooled constantly, and her nose was always runny.

Her suction machine was our best friend, although she frowned every time she heard it power up. It kept her nasal passage and mouth clear of thick mucus. Dr. Waki recommended a minor procedure that would help with her secretions. He put tubes in her ears with the hope of decreasing the secretion flow from her nose and mouth. Unfortunately, we really didn't see a big difference but continued to trust God.

Appointments flowed continuously. The life of a "Career Wife/Mother" changed drastically. I never thought that I would be a stay-at-home mom. God knows best!

On August 8, we decided to dedicate Genesis to the Lord with a formal christening. We asked Dr. Sloan to be her Godfather a few months after she was born. What better person to ask than the doctor who saved both of our lives? He accepted without any hesitation and said it would be an honor.

Sister Joyce graciously accepted our request to be Genesis' Godmother as she provided spiritual literature and weekly prayers the

Sentenced to Live

entire pregnancy. Our parents flew in from Louisiana to witness this awesome occasion. It was the second Sunday of the month, and the Voices of Joy choir was ministering in song. The praise service was so uplifting. Pastor approached the podium and said, "I know you are trying to figure out what's going on in this service, and why no one can sit down this morning. Church, Genesis Jones is in the house." The entire congregation went into a serious praise and worship service. Members were crying uncontrollably with joy because the miracle baby was in attendance. Our church prayed for her non-stop during this tough journey. God answered our prayers. What a blessing it was to see the manifestation of our prayers right before our very eyes.

Chapter Ten

First Birthday

A few months later, I received a call from our pastor sharing what the Lord placed on his heart. He said that God told him to hire me as his pastoral executive assistant.

I was speechless as he was talking. I thought, *who is going to take care of my baby?* He said, "The best news of all is that you can bring her to work with you, and you only have to come on Tuesdays, Wednesdays, Thursdays, and Sundays. You only have to come when I'm in the office."

Sentenced to Live

Greg and I were so excited. We would all be working together at the church. It couldn't get any better than that. Of course, our pastor and everyone on staff knew our situation, so it was perfect.

It was a huge blessing and an honor to serve as his assistant. I took that job very seriously and enjoyed serving under his leadership.

Genesis had a blast going to work with us. She sat in her colorful, toddler rocker watching TV or was stretched out in front of Pastor's desk in her portable playpen. Genesis became spoiled rotten.

Pastor's "co-assistant" had her own unique, spiritual way of letting him know how his day would go. They had a special way of communicating with each other.

Sorry, I'm not privileged to share confidential information. Genesis attended every meeting, church service, and some

Sentenced to Live

outings. During this period, we were able to sign her up for therapy sessions at a school near the church on the days that I worked.

Greg's office was upstairs next door to her Godmother. Therefore, she spent a lot of time around people who prayed for her and loved her dearly.

After being employed for several months, the Lord blessed us with part-time nursing care to assist with Genesis, which meant she didn't have to travel to work with us as often.

Genesis truly enjoyed attending worship services every Sunday. She always thought Pastor was speaking directly to her when he was preaching.

This was absolutely hilarious! There were several occasions when he said something directly to her because she may have been a little irritable. He would say, "Genesis,

Poppee is talking, be nice" and she would settle down. She knew his voice.

Ironically, she would do the same thing if her dad was singing or directing the choir. There is nothing like a daddy's girl.

Genesis celebrated her first birthday a few months after I started working at the church. Planning her first birthday party was very emotional for us. The invitation read "It's a day of Thanksgiving and Praise in honor of my first birthday" with a picture of Genesis wrapped in shiny, gold fabric with matching wings.

One of the church members reserved the recreation center in Placentia. Princess Genesis wore a beautiful green and yellow two-piece outfit with a matching ruffled hat. Several hundred guests greeted her.

Various individuals spoke about what Genesis' testimony meant to them. From around the world, many walked this journey

Sentenced to Live

with us. Celebrating this day was very special as she was sentenced to death upon arrival, but God had other plans. Our precious baby girl was one year old! I felt like running a few victory laps.

Sentenced to Live

Chapter Eleven

School Days

G enesis was approaching three years old when we were told that she could attend a special needs school near our home. If your child is under the age of 3 and has a disability, he or she may be eligible for services from a Regional Center through California's Early Start program.

Special education gives instruction and supports that are specially designed to meet the unique needs of a child whose disability affects his or her educational performance or ability to learn in a regular classroom.

Sentenced to Live

These special services are provided at no cost because state and federal law requires that all children in public schools who are eligible for special education receive a free and appropriate public education. A child who is eligible may receive a variety of services, including speech and language therapy, psychological services, physical and occupational therapy, and counseling services. The child may also receive transportation and other supports needed to access and benefit from his or her education. (2018 ca.gov).

Genesis received transporting services. Her regular stroller was not sufficient enough to transport her to school.

She was examined and fitted for her first custom made wheelchair. It was navy blue with strong, steady wheels. A high-powered stroller tailor made for a princess.

As you can imagine, it was difficult to release her to attend preschool, but we knew this

Sentenced to Live

was best for her. Greg struggled greatly with this decision. Of course, we were entrusting our three-year old, non-verbal, and wheelchair-bound daughter into the hands of strangers four hours daily for a few days a week.

The school program was formulated for five days per week, but Greg was not in agreement; he wanted her to go to school only a few days. I was not totally comfortable but knew it was the best thing for her physical, emotional, and mental development.

Prior to her starting, we had an opportunity to visit her school and meet with the principal, staff, and teacher. Her teacher, Ms. Rhonda, assured me that she would be attending the best school in America. She made several visits to our home to make us feel more relaxed.

Genesis rode the bus to and from school and really enjoyed the ride. Her teacher said she cried a few times a day but we knew she would grow to love it, and she did. We were so grateful for an awesome public special needs school that had a complete package of qualified staff to care for her. We received a detailed daily report that summarized Genesis' day and described how she accomplished her IEP (Individualized Educational Program) goals.

Once a child is found eligible for special education, parents participate in the process by attending an IEP meeting at the child's school at least once a year.

At this meeting, parents and other members of the team write an IEP plan that describes the child's educational needs and the services that will be provided to meet those needs (2018 ca.gov) . The daily report included the number of times her diaper was changed, her mood – happy or sad –and so much more!

Chapter Twelve

Genesis Choices

We were outgrowing our space and needed a home that would accommodate Genesis as she grew. The time had come for to us purchase a larger home with multiple bedrooms on the main floor.

The housing market was very lucrative in 2002, so we decided to sell our townhome. It took us a few weeks to find a place. I told my realtor that I wanted to acknowledge and honor Genesis' reactions when we found the place that we liked.

Sentenced to Live

We took Genesis to tour two homes. She cried and was uncomfortable in the first home. We didn't stay long at all. Visiting the second home was very interesting. The homeowners could not leave due to their sick child and asked if they could stay during our visit. Normally, sellers don't stay in the home while a potential buyer is viewing. We found the family to be very interesting. Genesis laughed during the whole visit.

The male homeowner asked, "What do you need me to do to accommodate your daughter in this home?" I was shocked and in disbelief that he was asking me these questions.

I said, "Let me think about it." He asked if we were preapproved. I answered, "Yes, we are approved, Sir." We continued to view the home and took notes. I was surprised to hear that he was a contractor.

How about that! We placed an offer and listed a few things that we would like

Sentenced to Live

completed due to an unfinished room. He fixed EVERYTHING and added a new countertop in the kitchen. He told our realtor that he wanted our daughter to be comfortable in her new home. Who does that? A man after God's own heart.

A few weeks after moving into our home, we received a knock on the door from one of our neighbors welcoming us to the neighborhood.

They dropped off some homemade cookies and wanted to meet Genesis. It took us a while to get her out of the car, and I'm sure the neighbors were observing from their windows.

However, this particular family chose to take a different route. I was so impressed with them. They truly epitomized the scripture "As for me and my house, we will serve the Lord."

Sentenced to Live

All of the kids were homeschooled and loved
the Lord just as much as their parents.
Periodically, one of the children would
knock on the door and ask if I needed help
with anything or simply wanted to stop by
to see how Genesis was doing.

Chapter Thirteen

The Seizure

Our family was enjoying a nice, warm late summer evening when we noticed that Genesis was having a seizure. It was scary. She stopped breathing and turned blue.

OMG! Where did this come from? We gave her a dose of diastat and administered CPR immediately. Lord Jesus! I could not believe this was happening. It's not normal practice to give mouth-to-mouth during a seizure because most people start to breathe on their own. However, our situation was different from the normal with Genesis' critical medical background of not breathing on her own as an infant.

We drove two blocks down the street to the ER. It was too close to wait on the paramedics. The doctors ran several tests to be sure she was stable before they released her.

Greg started singing her favorite song, "Balm in Gilead" and she cracked a little smile. Genesis fell in love with this song when she was only a few months old. Greg and I bought the live video recording of this song by Karen Clark Sheard and watched it frequently. Genesis always smiled when she heard this song. It made her happy.

That smile was confirmation that she was going to be fine. Thank you, God! She was transferred to St. Jude in Fullerton late that evening per orders from her pediatrician. She was admitted for a few days for further observation.

Sentenced to Live

Her doctor suggested an EEG to determine how often the seizures were occurring. Results showed seizures were frequent. The dosage was increased with the hopes of the seizures lessening. We didn't want her to have large doses due to the side effects. Seizure medication has its advantages and disadvantages. The number one advantage is that it treats seizures and decreases the occurrence. Some disadvantages are drowsiness, dizziness, mood and behavior swings.

Genesis' hospitalization at St. Jude brought back so many memories. Gen was in the fight of her life a few years prior. This was not a place where we wanted to be for a long period of time. Our stay was not long at all.

The Lord continued to bless us in spite of it all, so we could be a blessing to Genesis and each other. The opportunities were God-sent. We were in need of medical benefits with no pre-existing clauses. I applied for a

Sentenced to Live

job that had nothing to do with my college degree, but the company had great medical benefits with flexibility that would allow me to continually be an active part of my daughter's care. I recall going to the interview in San Diego to meet with the hiring manager. Preparing for the interview was intense, as I had no experience in this area.

I arrived ready to take on several rounds of questions, and to my surprise, the manager wanted to know about my daughter. He said, "I've heard so much about your daughter through your friend. Tell me about her. What's her diagnosis?" We spoke for at least thirty minutes about our children. He asked what day of the week I needed off for therapy and what hours were preferable. I sat in a state of shock, asking myself if this was a real interview or a joke.

He ended the interview by saying, "We would love to have you. If you have time,

can you drive to the corporate office in Santa
Ana and meet the vice president of
marketing?" Of course, I said, "Yes, no
problem at all." I drove to Santa Ana and
met the VP of marketing. We spoke for
twenty minutes, and I received a call a few
days later with my start date. That was the
easiest job interview I ever had. The
founding president of the company was a
family man and believed in work-life
balance. In addition, Greg was offered a
position at a church in the Los Angeles area
where the pastor was passionate and
humble.

Sentenced to Live

Chapter Fourteen

Trials to Ministry

The journey continued as we faced trials and tests with Genesis' health. The doctor appointments, therapy sessions, durable medical equipment, and clinics never ceased. Our life reminded me of Eleanor Roosevelt's quote, "People are like tea bags. You never how strong they are until you put them in hot water." Although, it was not hot water, it truly was a test of our faith in God. Greg's mind and heart was flooded with new songs and music during this phase of our lives. He handpicked over 30 God-fearing members to form his choir

Sentenced to Live

"Ministry." The debut concert was beyond phenomenal. He ministered mightily under the direction of the Holy Spirit, encouraging the attendees that God had a blessing for them and dared them to turn it over to the Lord and watch their prayer request become their praise report. He also shared that God remembered every trial, tribulation, and circumstance, and will walk you through each struggle. We minister in song throughout the country.

Ministry toured our home state Memorial Day weekend in 2005 and ministered at my home church Elm Grove and Beacon Light in New Orleans. I recall watching the news when I heard that Hurricane Katrina was headed to Louisiana. The beauty of hurricanes is that you normally receive an advance warning a few days prior to their arrival. Most of our family was prepared. Some went to higher ground and others stayed put. Hurricane Katrina made landfall along the gulf coast with winds over 100

Sentenced to Live

mph and stretched across over 400 miles. This was the beginning of pain and suffering in the bayou. I was at work right when the storm arrived. I and one of my colleagues, who is a native of New Orleans, embraced each other in the hallway as we watched the news about our birthplace. This storm brought so many people together. Several days went by without hearing from our family members. Every time we called there was a busy signal, or we would get a message stating that all circuits were busy. We prayed and promised to keep each other lifted in prayer and provide support until we heard from our families. None of Ministry choir members could have visualized that Hurricane Katrina would come along months later and drown the beautiful sanctuary of Beacon Light where we ministered in song months ago with thirteen feet of water.

The church was left with over one million dollars in damage. Our hearts was broken to hear of numerous friends, family and church communities who suffered greatly during this time.

After much thought and prayer, Greg and I decided to relocate back to Louisiana two years after the storm. Genesis was around eight years old and it was the perfect season to spend more time with her grandparents and extended family. My company's executive management team supported me in my transfer to the Louisiana office as an assistant project manager. I assisted families of Louisiana affected by Hurricanes Katrina and Rita to settle back in their homes. Oh what a joy it was to help my community! Greg was blessed with an awesome opportunity as well.

Our miracle child was able to enroll in school and met a phenomenal teacher, Mrs. East. She was a seasoned teacher with splendid knowledge on assisting kids with

Sentenced to Live

special needs. Genesis swept us all off of our feet as she was featured in *Baton Rouge Parents Magazine* as a cover kid. The interview process was a fun-filled day of events. I was determined to stand in line and get her in front of the panel of judges. Inclusion was my new middle name. I made a promise to God that I would never allow her to be excluded from any events that involve children her age. There were two other special needs students present, but I was positively sure that she would be selected.

Not only was she selected to be in the magazine that year, but she also spoke her first words at school. We were overjoyed to hear the news. Her child specific aide recorded her saying "it's ok" to someone in the class. What's ironic is that I shared those exact words with my aunt several times when she came over that morning to assist with Gen, so I know she said it. The second time she spoke, she said "brother." Well,

Sentenced to Live

that's what we called my youngest brother frequently. Thirdly, she said, "I love you." I love you was definitely words she heard from our family all the time. I actually heard her say it a few times. Talk about melodies from heaven.

Chapter Fifteen

Going back to Cali

Unfortunately, our tenure in Louisiana was short. Our families were heartbroken but understood our circumstances. The project I was working on ended and I was being transferred back to California. However, it was a promotion to client project manager. Greg was blessed once again and walked right back into the position he had prior to us leaving California at First AME. On top of all of that, our daughter was able to attend her old school without hesitation.

Sentenced to Live

We moved back when Gen was just shy of being a teenager. Although she progressed in Louisiana, the school in California was more equipped and the medical services were vaster. We pulled up to the school on her first day back and she started cracking up laughing. I think she knew where she was. This gave Greg and I relief that we made the right decision.

Her old teachers and principal kept in touch, which allowed the transition to be smooth. A few years passed and our Genesis was approaching her sixteenth birthday. I had big ideas of planning this huge celebration with a nice sit-down dinner decorated with elegant table and chair coverings. Greg stopped me in my tracks and said, "Why we would spend money on plated meals when our daughter can't partake due to her being fed via g-tube. Let's do something that she would really enjoy. How about a musical?"

Sentenced to Live

I said, "Bey, you are a genius, that's it." We solicited help from a few friends who called themselves "Gen's Dream Team." They helped set up, decorate, take photos, break down, etc. The musical was held at Friendship Baptist Church where her journey started 16 years prior. We invited choirs from our church, First AME (FAME) Church of Los Angeles so she would have some of her favorites in attendance. Each choir had to sing two of her favorite gospel songs. Her theme was "Melodies of a Miracle." She was laughing the entire afternoon. It was all about her. We had several family members fly in for the occasion and friends throughout Southern California. Everyone had an opportunity to have a slice of cake, pack a sweet treat from her sweet bar and take pictures with the guest of honor.

Gen did not stop there. I mentioned that my new nickname was inclusion. Well Genesis was recommended by a friend to interview

Sentenced to Live

as a debutante for Alpha Kappa Alpha Sorority, Inc. Only those applicants with outstanding qualifications would be considered. We accompanied her to the interview. There was a panel of individuals from the sorority asking us questions about her accomplishments at school and in the community. Her highlights were not like the other young ladies. However, we gladly stated that she received student of the month multiple times for communication skills, 100 mile club, her success with her IEP goals, and other activities. Greg and I shared that "we live in a society where barriers and walls are being torn down every day to include special needs individuals nationwide on different levels.

This will truly be an awesome honor for her and as parents we strive hard to be certain that she experiences what every young woman her age has the desire to achieve." We also shared that "she received a personal congratulatory 16th birthday message from

Sentenced to Live

the 44th President of the United States, Barack and First Lady Michelle Obama and we would be forever grateful for their thoughtfulness if selected as a debutante."

The committee stated they would notify us by letter of the results. After their statement Gen let out a small gesture, as to say, your notification will be a yes. Everyone in the room chuckled. Genesis was selected as the first special needs debutante for that chapter. It was an experience of a lifetime. The young ladies who were juniors and seniors in high school fell in love with Genesis. They learned a lot about our beautiful young lady who could not walk, talk or eat on her own.

 She fell in love with them and they were elated to have her around. She was not able to participate in all of the events planned during the season. This was certainly our choice! I recalled during the talent portion at one of the events that each girl had to

Sentenced to Live

display their talent. I got permission from the president of the chapter and asked Gen's principal, teacher and physical education coordinator to bring her gait trainer. Her dad played "Smile" by Kirk Franklin as she took a few steps for the girls to show her skills. There was not a dry face in the room. Her debutante sisters were crying, floored and cheered her as she took those steps with assistance.

The dance routines were choreographed to include her in every routine the night of the ball. I think one of her favorite routines was to Beyoncé's "Run the World." The father-daughter dance was my favorite as her dad had to improvise during curtsy by tilting her wheelchair back and forth during the routine. It was a beautiful night indeed.

Chapter Sixteen

Stay Close

As I share a glimpse of our journey, I realize that many years have elapsed since I began writing this book. My Genesis is now 20. She normalized my husband's and my life. Our losses were life changing, life threatening, and life provoking all at the same time. All the loss in that short period of time is consoled by her beautiful, unconditional and redemptive love. Every time I look at her or embrace and kiss her, and she embraces me back, I see plainly the hand of God in my life. It's time for me to share. Healing has given birth to purpose,

Sentenced to Live

and the purpose of my life is to share with anyone who may be at this juncture of loss. The pain is no longer painful but now a testimony.

Currently, our beautiful miracle baby Genesis is a vibrant, young woman. Greg and I have been blessed to care for her at the most pivotal milestones in her life. All these memories are filled with some clouds and lots of sunshine provided by the hand of our Lord. His grace and mercy have lifted us when life's storms would have surely taken us under. Although Greg and I have been through so much, there is still more to tell.

There have been many seasons that we gazed into the unknown and asked the Lord, what's next? Not knowing the innocence of our question, it was truly His mercies and grace that sustained us. I am a mother who is dealing with the fact that I am caring for my daughter who without another miracle from God will never be able to care for

Sentenced to Live

herself or have a child of her own. This brings reality front and center to me. I am also acutely aware of the fact that God has given me beauty for ashes and awakened a stirring within my spirit.

I feel as though I have a spiritual baby inside my belly that leaps at the notion that I have been called to mend the broken hearted and to feed our Lord's sheep. My Master and Savior has given me a message that I must proclaim from an altar that once was a place of sacrifice for me and my husband. Stay close! I will be in touch with you to share more. Until then, remember that God will never allow life to give you more than you can bear (1 Corinthians 10:13).

About the Author

Alicia S. Jones is a Louisiana native who resides in the Los Angeles, California area. She is the chief operating officer and director of events for Smokey Note Entertainment and vice president of Southern University Alumni, Los Angeles Chapter. In addition, she is the girl's varsity volleyball coach at Vineyard Christian School and a volunteer for Forever Footprints organization.

Alicia is a member of First AME Church (FAME) Los Angeles. She earned a Bachelor of Science in psychology from Southern University A&M College (Baton Rouge). She has been happily married to her husband Gregory for 28 years, and they are proud parents of their special needs angel, Genesis.